# YOURS IS A SHARE

# Yours is a Share

## The Call of Liturgical Ministry

AUSTIN FLEMING

The Pastoral Press
Washington, D.C.

ISBN: 0-912405-20-1

Copyright © 1985, The Pastoral Press. All Rights Reserved.

The Pastoral Press
225 Sheridan Street, NW
Washington, DC 20011
(202) 723-5800

The Pastoral Press is the publications division of the National Association of Pastoral Musicians, a membership organization of musicians and clergy dedicated to fostering the art of musical liturgy.

Printed in the United States of America

Typography & Design: Paul Gunzelmann
Lincoln Graphics/Washington

# CONTENTS

PREFACE  *1*

THE MINISTRY OF THE ASSEMBLY  *3*

THE MINISTRY OF THE LITURGY TEAM  *7*

THE MINISTRY OF HOSPITALITY  *11*

THE MINISTRY OF MUSIC  *15*

THE PRESIDER'S MINISTRY  *21*

THE LECTOR'S MINISTRY  *27*

THE MINISTRY OF PREACHING  *31*

THE MINISTERS OF DANCED PRAYER  *37*

THE MINISTERS OF THE EUCHARIST  *41*

# PREFACE

Our true friends are those rare individuals who bring the right mix of support and challenge into our lives, who know us well enough that every time we spend time with them, we know better who we are.

This book has become a true friend for many persons. It started out as part of a larger work, *Preparing for Liturgy: A Theology and Spirituality*, by Austin Fleming. It remains part of that work, but while it was in the process of growing from manuscript to book, I had occasions to use these pages in many workshops on liturgy and ministry in parishes and dioceses. As I would close a session that dealt with one of the specific ministries, always trying to unite that ministry to the ONE ministry that is ours, I would offer the appropriate reflection.

From Minnesota to Florida, from Maryland to Alabama, persons asked for a copy of "the blessing" or "the challenge" that I had read for them. It is these persons who convinced me again that too often we deal with our ministers in terms of schedules, behavior, cooperation— all important aspects of ministry in the liturgy—but we rarely talk with these persons about the heart of the matter, as a true friend would, blessing and challenging, reminding them of who they are and who they are called to be.

This book is offered for all those persons, the hundreds who share in the Lord's ministry to the Christian community week after week.

Just as these reflections were originally offered, they appear here not in an order of importance, but in the order in which these ministries touch the prayer of God's people. At least once, resist the temptation to skip to the section that refers to the service you offer, and read through the whole. Appreciate that you are, first and foremost, a member of the assembly. Take time to unite your ministry with the assembly's ministry as well as with those who minister within the Sunday Eucharist.

On some days, the reflection may be supportive of your work. On another, it may be more of a challenge. Whether this is a "blessing day" or a "challenge day" it is hoped that these reflections will continue to be helpful in refreshing and renewing your ministry. As each reflection closes: "Be faithful in the work you do, for through it the Lord saves his people."

Mary Ellen Cohn
Editor

# THE MINISTRY OF THE ASSEMBLY

Yours is a share
in the work
of the Spirit of all that is holy,
for in who you are
and in what you do
is found the most powerful
experience of the sacred.

Yours is the kingdom community
whose very assembling
is sacrament of God's presence in the world.

In the living words, gestures, sacrifice,
and meal of your common prayer,
the living God is disclosed
as the faithful and redeeming Lord
whose tent is pitched among us.

Yours is to be nothing more
and nothing less than the body of Christ.

Yours is the ministry of being the beloved
and espoused of God.

Through your lives and in your midst
the tidings of salvation
are faithfully proclaimed.

Yours is the work of telling and handing on
the story of God's mercy.

You are the people
who embody the promise of life forever.

For the world you are evidence
that the word of judgment
is tempered with compassion.

**Yours is the ministry
of celebrating again and again
the Passover meal of the new Covenant.**

**Your sacrifice of praise
is a hymn to the Lamb of God
who takes away the sins of the world.**

**Yours is the work
of gathering at that table which welcomes all
who turn their hearts back to God.**

**Yours is the ministry to bring bread and wine,
to give thanks,
to break and share the bread,
to bless and share the cup
—remembering Christ Jesus
broken and poured out for your sakes.**

**Yours is the proclamation of the
'mysterium fidei', the mystery of faith.**

**Come to your ministry
from your personal prayer:
it is the home from which you journey
to the house of God's people,
to the tables of their common prayer.**

**Come prepared to be surprised
by God's word and presence
in the assembly of your neighbors.**

**Come as you are!
Come as sinners
who need to find mercy,
as the redeemed who need to give thanks.**

Come with all that needs to be healed,
to the Lord who comes to heal you.

Come with no expectations,
save the sure hope of communion
with the Holy One
in the family of God's people.

If your community's liturgy
is alive and beautiful,
take care
lest you begin to worship your worship:
this is idolatry.

If your community's liturgy
needs help—offer it!

Model your community's liturgy
on Christ's divine service,
not on the experience of neighboring parishes.

The liturgy your parish offers
is often a mirror of the life your parish lives:
look into that mirror
and see what you will see;
then do what must be done.

When visitors praise and thank you
for the worship you have offered,
take delight in the blessing
they have received,
and rejoice in the work
the Lord has accomplished through you.

Be faithful in the work you do,
for through it the Lord saves his people.

# THE MINISTRY OF THE LITURGY TEAM

Yours is a share
in the work of the Lord's Spirit
who calls God's people to prayer.

You help prepare the way of the Lord
who comes with mercy and with peace.

Yours is the guardianship of that holy ground
where God and God's people meet
and sit at a common table.

Yours is the work
of preparing the table of the Lord
who is our Passover.

Yours is the task of calling others
to serve at that table,
and of preparing them
to serve with grace and reverence.

Yours is the task
of helping God's people to shape a prayer
that they might sing from their hearts.

Yours is nothing less
than the responsibility of insuring
that God's word is proclaimed,
clearly and with conviction.

Come to your work
from your personal prayer;
begin your work together
with prayer in common.

Let your meetings be long enough
to do the work that is yours to do,
but not so long
as to go beyond where the Spirit leads you.

Root your meetings
in the scriptures of the liturgy you prepare,
for the prayer of that celebration
will be rooted in God's word.

Let your meetings be marked
by a unity in spirit and in ideals.

As others are called by the Lord,
invite them to join in your work.

Remember
that the treasure of the prayer of God's people
is one you hold in an earthen vessel.

Be gentle,
and reverence what is entrusted to you.

Let this treasure
bear the imprint of your community,
but take care
lest it be smudged by your fingers.

Should your zeal
sometime marr or crack this treasure,
do not panic.

Acknowledge and study the error,
remembering that the Lord will heal
what you have broken:
learn, as we all do, from your mistakes.

When your brothers and sisters
thank and praise you for your work,
take delight
in a prayer that has touched their hearts,
and rejoice in the work
the Lord has accomplished through you.

Be faithful in the work you do,
for through it the Lord saves his people.

# THE MINISTRY OF HOSPITALITY

**Yours is the first of Christ's faces**
**to greet God's people**
**as they assemble for prayer.**

**Your greeting of welcome**
**is the first wish that "The Lord be with you!"**

**Yours is the word**
**that welcomes the stranger to be at home,**
**or the silence**
**that makes of our assembly a foreign land.**

**Yours is the task of discretion:**
**knowing how to welcome, and,**
**when and where, to seat the latecomer.**

**Yours may be the last word**
**that ushers the community**
**to its week of work in the Lord's vineyard.**

**Yours is the Lord's face and voice**
**for those who enter and depart**
**the holy ground of prayer.**

Come to your work and your post
from your personal prayer;
be as ready as the Lord to meet his people.

Let your welcome and your smile
be for all who enter;
remember that you will have time
to see your close friends later in the week.

Seek out the lost and the confused;
do not wait for them to come to you.

When appropriate,
lend a hand and an arm to the disabled,
remembering your own infirmities.

Greet each person as the Lord,
for that is precisely whom you meet.

When taking up the collection,
remember
that it is for the work of God's people,
especially among the poor;
remember, too,
that many who make an offering
are themselves the poor.

Remember that you stand at the temple gates:
some will come rejoicing,
and others in fear;
some will come healed,
and others to seek that healing.

Be sensitive,
and welcome all as best you can.

Some will rush by and ignore you:
let go of your disappointment
and pray for the Lord's gentle touch
on their heavy or hurried hearts.

Some may fall ill while at prayer:
see to their needs
as you would have them see to yours.

Be slow to judge those who leave early:
be glad that they have shared in our prayer
and recall that only the Lord
knows the reasons of the heart.

When your brothers and sisters
thank and praise you for your work,
take delight
in the welcome they have found,
and rejoice in the work
the Lord has accomplished through you.

Be faithful in the work you do,
for through it the Lord saves his people.

# THE MINISTRY OF MUSIC

Yours is a share
in the work of the Lord's Spirit
who draws us together into one,
who makes harmony out of discord,
who sings in our hearts
the lyric of all that is holy.

Yours is the joy of sounding that first note
which brings the assembly to its feet,
ready to praise God.

Yours is to impart
a "quality of joy and enthusiasm"
[that] cannot be gained in any other way."

Yours is a ministry
that reaches the deepest recesses
of the human heart;
your work is soul-stirring.

Yours is none other than the Lord's song;
you draw us into that canticle of divine praise
sung throughout the ages
in the halls of heaven.

You help us to respond to God's word,
to acclaim the gospel,
to sing of our salvation in Christ.

Yours is a ministry
that gathers our many voices
into one grand choir of praise.

Come to your work
from your personal prayer.

Let your rehearsals begin
with prayer in common.
Let your practice be marked
by unanimity in spirit and in ideals.

Be gentle in correcting one another:
the kingdom will not fall on a flatted note.

Open your choir to those
whom the Lord has blessed with musical gift;
help the not so gifted
to discern the talents that are theirs.

Rehearse the Lord's song
with the reverence it is due.

Take care
to study the scriptures for the liturgy
in which you will serve;
know well the word that calls forth our praise.

Let the lyrics of your songs be strong,
true, and rooted in the scriptures;
those who sing the Lord's word
sing the Lord's song.

Make no room for the trite,
the maudlin, the sentimental.

Open your hearts and voices
to new songs
worthy of God's people at prayer.

Let your repertoire change
as all living things must,
but not so much
that the song of God's people is lost.

Be ambitious for the higher gifts,
but not beyond your gifts;
respect the range of talent
the Lord has given you and your community.

Think first of the assembly's song,
for this is the song you serve.

Let your music
be always the servant of the Lord,
of God's people,
of the divine service they offer.

Let the service of your music
always complement
but never overshadow
the people's ritual prayer.

Let your performance become a prayer,
and your art a gift.

Let technique become no idol,
but simply a tool
for honing the beauty of your gift.

Remember that your ministry
is ever an emptying out of yourself;
when the solo is assigned to another,
let that singer's offering
become your prayer.

When no one comments on the new motet,
be thankful that your work
led the people to God,
not to you.

When the assembly will not sing,
be patient with them
and with yourselves;
the Lord's song is sometimes a quiet one
and silence precedes every hymn.

Waste no time wondering,
"Do you think they liked it?"
but ask at all times,
"Did it help them and all of us to pray?"

When your ministry leads you to music,
it has led you astray.

When your ministry leads you to the Lord,
it has brought you home.

When your brothers and sisters
thank and praise you for your work,
take delight
in the song their prayer has become,
and rejoice in the work
the Lord has accomplished through you.

Be faithful in the work you do,
for through it the Lord saves his people.

# THE PRESIDER'S MINISTRY

Yours is a share
in the work of the Lord's Spirit
who gathers us from east to west
to make an offering of praise
to the glory of God's holy name.

Yours is the task
of calling us to remember God's mercy
and our need for it.

Yours is the voice
that calls us to hear God's holy word,
and to share
in the meal of the Lord's supper.

You "collect" our many prayers
and make them one
in our prayer as church.

With us,
and in our name,
you take bread and wine,
you speak our thanks to God,
break the bread of life
and share with us the cup of salvation.

Yours is to preside
over the great thanksgiving
of God's people in Christ.

Come to your work
from your personal prayer;
your public prayer with the community
depends on this.

Come to the liturgy
steeped in the scriptures of the day
lest your presidency be illiterate.

Come to the place of prayer early;
enter freely and peacefully
upon that holy ground
lest your ministry be hasty or unprepared.

Come to your ministry as do all God's people:
deeply aware
of your need for the Lord's mercy.

Depend on and allow the other ministers
to offer their services
as they have been called to do.

Let them be your fellow ministers,
not personal aides or underlings.

Be gentle
when correction is needed.

Remember that the liturgy
is the assembly's prayer;
because you are one with them,
it is yours too.

Call your fellow ministers
to faithfulness and preparedness
by the model of your own work.
Ask not of others
what you do not demand of yourself.

Let every prayer and word you speak
from chair, ambo, and table
be clear, strong, and true.

Trust always in the Spirit,
but not too much in your own spontaneity;
even the poet writes many drafts
before the final verse.

Anyone can read texts;
only the believer can pray them.

<u>Pray</u> the prayers
and <u>proclaim</u> the scriptures!

Let all your movement and gesture
be strong, graceful, and with purpose;
the hurried step is distracting,
and the weak gesture insignificant.

Let nothing be affected;
let everything be done with reverence.

Handle holy things with holy care.

Let your ministry
be emptied of self-interest.

Remember
that it is the assembly's prayer that you serve.

Think not of yourself
as the center of things
but as the one who helps keep things centered
—on the Lord.

Let your eyes fall often on God's people
as the eyes of the servant
are on the hands of the master.

Minister according to the customs
of the church,
and not by personal taste;
this prayer belongs to the people
and they trust it to your care.

Let the liturgy be your prayer,
lest the celebration space become your stage.

When your brothers and sisters
praise and thank you for your work,
delight in the rite
that has become their prayer
and rejoice in the work
the Lord has accomplished through you.

Be faithful in the work you do,
for through it the Lord saves his people.

# THE LECTOR'S MINISTRY

Yours is a share
in the work of the Lord's Spirit
who opens our hearts to God's holy word.

Yours is the task of telling our family story,
the story of salvation.

Yours is to proclaim
the true and saving word of God.

You are the messenger of God's love for us.

Your task is to proclaim that word,
which challenges, confronts,
and captures our hearts.

You proclaim a word
that heals and comforts and consoles.

Yours is the ministry
of the table of God's word,
which feeds the hungers and the longing
of our hearts for truth.

Yours is to offer the story
of the "great things the Lord has done for us,"
that we might turn to the table of eucharist
with good cause to give thanks and praise.

Yours is nothing less
than the ministry of the Lord's voice
calling out in the midst of God's people.

Come to your work
from your personal prayer,
praying that the Spirit
will open your heart to what you proclaim.

Prepare the word which is yours to speak:
study the scriptures,
understand the passage,
let it dwell deep within you.

Come to your work in awesome reverence
of the word you proclaim:
it is the Lord's word.

Come to your ministry
as one judged and saved
by the word you speak.

Anyone can read the scriptures in public;
only the believer can proclaim them.

Approach the ambo,
the table of the Lord's word,
as you would the Lord himself:
with reverence and awe.

Handle the book of the Lord's word
with great care:
it is a tabernacle of the Lord's presence.

Let your eyes fall often
on the faces of the assembly:
they are the body of the Lord
whose word you proclaim.

Let the Lord's peace settle in your heart,
that your voice may be clear and steady.

Let your voice echo the sound of the word,
with conviction, with gentleness,
with strength, and with wonder.

Remember that the story you tell
is filled with a drama you need not supply,
but must always convey.

Like the prophet,
you will sometimes proclaim
what no one wants to hear;
remember always
your own need to hear the hard saying,
and never imagine that your ministry
places you above what you proclaim.

If you are the best of the parish lectors,
be gentle in helping others to improve.

If you are the least of the parish lectors,
seek out that help which others can give.

If you do not know how well you read—ask:
be grateful for constructive criticism
and humbled by any praise your receive.

Every lector wants to read at the Easter Vigil
but not all will be assigned:
be patient in waiting your turn
and nourished by the word
that others proclaim.

Let no minister of the word
think that there is nothing left to learn:
another commentary and another workshop
cannot but help the open mind and heart.

When your brothers and sisters
praise and thank you for your work,
take delight in the word they have heard
and rejoice in the work
the Lord has accomplished through you.
Be faithful in the work you do,
for through it the Lord saves his people.

# THE MINISTRY OF PREACHING

Yours is a share
in the work of the Lord's Spirit
who opens our hearts
to the Good News of salvation.

Yours is the ministry
of the table of God's word.

Yours is the work
of breaking open the scriptures
that God's people might be nourished
by the food of the Lord's word.

Yours is the ministry of Jesus
who came to announce
that the reign of God is at hand.

Yours is the voice
which opens the challenge and the consolation
of the gospel in the parables of your homily.

Yours is to tell a story
that tells the story of God's love for us.

Yours is the prophet's ministry
among the home town folks.

Yours is the task
of announcing promise when hope is gone,
love when it has cooled,
justice to the oppressed and the oppressors,
joy when tears run freely,
and God when we are less than human.

Come to your work
from your personal prayer,
come filled with the word
that judges and saves your own life.

Bear the book of the gospels
as the weight of God's judgment
and the breath of God's mercy.

Bear this book as the ark of the covenant
—with reverence, awe, and wonder.

Proclaim the gospel
as if our lives depended on it:
they do.

Proclaim the Good News
as though we had never heard it:
we are slow to understand.

Prepare your proclamation of the gospel
as carefully as you prepare your homily:
the one will never fail,
the other may be forgotten.

Come to your preaching task
ever mindful of your own need
to hear the gospel message:
when you do this,
your word is clear and true.

Preach the <u>gospel</u>:
this is all we need to hear.

Pray for God's Spirit
that your mind and heart
be enlightened by the Light of Christ.

Let your preaching speak to this age,
but not be conformed to it;
let your thoughts be transformed
by the renewal of your mind in Christ Jesus,
and we shall be recreated.

Preach to us
as people you have come to know;
we know you so well by what you preach.

Struggle as you must
when preaching the difficult text
or the hard saying:
your honest struggle helps us in our own.

Spare us the used homily
when the cycle comes 'round again:
our lives have changed (as has your own)
and we hunger
for fresh food from the gospel table.

When the Lord has been sparing
of inspiration,
be brief:
we will understand.

Let not even your own sin
hold back from us the gospel's demands.

Preach the word in season and out of season,
yours and ours.

Do not shrink from naming what is sinful—
how else will we know our salvation?

Preach sin and grace
for this is what we know the best
and need to hear again.

Preach the reign of God in our midst:
help us to know its signs and presence.

Tell us the story of God's mercy:
no other story does as much.

Show us Jesus dying and rising among us:
this is what we have come here to see.

When your brothers and sisters
praise and thank you for your work,
take delight in the word
that has nourished them
and rejoice in the work
the Lord has accomplished through you.

Be faithful in the work you do,
for through it the Lord saves his people.

# THE MINISTERS OF DANCED PRAYER

Yours is a share
in the work of the Lord's Spirit
who is ever moving in our hearts
and among God's people.

You gesture with your whole selves
the prayer we know in our hearts:
with us and for us
you bring that prayer to living sign;
yours is a ministry of Word become flesh.

You move among us like God's own Spirit:
with beauty and strength;
with fire and peace;
with tenderness and power.

In all of this you lead us, in the Spirit,
to lift our hands and hearts
in praise of the living God.

Come to your work
from your personal prayer.

Come filled with the song, the Word,
and the silence of your prayer.

Let the dance of your own prayer
overflow in prayer and movement
for the assembled believers.

Please, do not come to dance for us;
come only to lead us in prayer
through the dance
that is your prayer for the Lord.

Prepare for your ministry
as the preacher prepares for the homily:
with time, energy, prayer, and work.

We are not interested
in your extemporaneous performance;
rather, dance for us and with us
the prayer you know by heart.

Understand that we will not always
understand your ministry.

Be patient with us, and help us to learn,
to appreciate the wonder
of all the gifts the Lord shares
through our brothers and sisters.

Teach us to pray with our whole selves,
and be patient with us
when we are awkward and embarrassed.

Be gentle in leading us and our prayer,
and the heart and flesh from which we pray.

Remember that your ministry
is a giving of self
and that your danced prayer
is uniquely a giving of your whole self
in the Lord's service.

More than most ministers,
you render your whole person and prayer
vulnerable to our critique
and misunderstanding.

Forgive us when we sin;
forgive our jealousy and pettiness.

Do not wonder if we enjoyed your dance;
rather, ponder how it has (or hasn't)
led us to pray with you.

When your brothers and sisters
praise and thank you for your work,
take delight in the prayer they have shared,
and be thankful for the work
the Lord has accomplished through your gift.

Be faithful in the work you do,
for through it the Lord saves his people.

# THE MINISTERS OF THE EUCHARIST

Yours is a share
in the work of the Lord's Spirit
who makes of us
one bread, one body,
the cup of blessing which we bless.

Yours is the work
of ministering Christ's body and blood
to the body of Christ, the church.

Yours is service
at the Lord's reconciling table.

You name for each of us
the gifts we have offered
and the gifts we receive:
"The Body of Christ, the Blood of Christ."

You minister holy food to holy people
in the holiest of all communions.

Yours is the ministry of the One
who was broken
and poured out for our sakes:
the ministry of Christ
who is our Passover and our lasting peace.

Come to your work
from your personal prayer,
praying that the Lord
will heal your brokenness
as you break and pour out
yourselves for others.

Remember the purity of the gifts you minister
and how great is your need
for the Lord's mercy.

Learn to love the eucharist you minister:
let it heal the hurt
your heart is slow to acknowledge;
let it make you one with all that is living;
let it help you revere
all those whom you serve.

Ministers of the eucharist are many;
truly eucharistic ministers
are what you must become.
Let your service at the Lord's table
make of your life
a table of mercy and welcome
for all you know and meet.

In and outside the worship space,
reverence those you serve
as you would reverence
the sacrament you minister.

When you minister to friends and family,
remember that the greatest bond you share
is in the Lord.

When you minister to visitors and strangers,
reverence them
as you would your closest friend.

When you minister
to those with whom you are at odds,
reverence them
as the Lord does you in your sin.

Some will esteem you as "holy"
because of the work you do:
remember
that your holiness
is the Lord's work within you.

When you are asked
to serve at inconvenient times,
let the needs of God's people
be your first consideration.

When you begin to think
that your ministry makes you
an important person in the community,
remember that what the Lord did at the table
became a sign of the Cross.

When your brothers and sisters
praise and thank you for your work,
take delight in the communion
you share with them in Christ
and rejoice in the work
the Lord has accomplished through you.

Be faithful in the work you do,
for through it the Lord saves his people.